PRAISE FC

MW01257321

"Claudia Putnam gives us the language to ask ourselves what we truly believe about the soul, suffering, and the value of life. As a parent called upon to make an unthinkable decision, she is a feeling and wise guide. *Double Negative* broke my heart and educated me."

—Pamela Erens, author of *Middlemarch and the Imperfect Life*

"*Double Negative* ushers us into the heart-wrenching grammar of loss, a warring opposition of 'worsts' wherein the only positive is possibility: a condition of suspended (non)being which 'isn't anyplace, and never was not.' Following Emerson and the probings of her heart, Claudia Putnam has spun a dazzlingly dark threnody into the labyrinth of love and grief, a journey deeply personal and, ultimately, for us all."

—Todd Hearon, author of *Strange Land* and *Crows in Eden*

"What a treasure, this memoir. With thoughtful and thought-provoking prose, Claudia Putnam tries to make sense of the senseless—the death of her newborn son, Jacob. Examining the intersection of life and death through many lenses, she considers ideas from the fields of literature and philosophy to physics and medical ethics, and she ponders deeply. Whether you're primarily a writer or a thinker, her words will inspire you to excel at both. And if you've made life-and-death medical decisions for your own newborn, you'll find comfort in knowing you're not alone in your search for answers and meaning."

—Deborah L. Davis, PhD, author of *Stillbirth, Yet Still Born* and *When Courage Lies in Letting Go*

"Heart-wrenching and unflinching, *Double Negative* explores powerful questions of how we define life's beginning and end, what a mother can know about a child in the womb, and the nature and existence of the soul. In telling the story of her infant son's death, Claudia Putnam brings a fierce intelligence to contemplating the decisions she made as a young mother and her perspective on those decisions now, thirty years later. *Double Negative* is an unforgettable wrestling with fundamental mysteries, a love song to a lost child that challenges our understanding of life and death."

—Katherine Towler, author of *The Penny Poet of Portsmouth*

""'Weepest thou?' Yes, and still": Three decades later, Claudia Putnam's *Double Negative* is an exquisite, evocative exploration of Self, Grief and the loss of a Soul that was destined to not be."

—Jonathan Chu, MD, Hospice Medical Director (retired)

DOUBLE NEGATIVE

DOUBLE NEGATIVE

A PERSONAL ESSAY BY

CLAUDIA PUTNAM

Thanks for checking This out ~

Portland Fest 11/24

SPLIT LIP
PRESS

Published by Split/Lip Press
6710 S. 87th St.
Ralston, NE 68127
www.splitlippress.com

ISBN: 978-1-952897-23-8

Cover Photograph: Valentin Lacoste
Cover and Book Design: David Wojciechowski
Editing: Lauren W. Westerfield

It is apparent there is no death
What is its significance?
—Edna St. Vincent Millay

To get born, your body makes a pact with death,
and from that moment, all it tries to do is cheat—
—Louise Glück

Three decades ago, my first son was born, and three days later, he died.

He died of a broken heart. He died in agony. He drowned in fluid backed up into his lungs. Because we couldn't speak to him, or because our culture tells us babies don't understand language, we watched, unable to communicate why this was happening to him, why we were letting this happen to him.

His name was Jacob, Jake. He came to an end in a round box carved from an aspen branch. Inside, a handful of white ash and bone.

Ash, less than for any of the dogs I've owned.

Ash, and a melted snap. From the onesie he wore into the oven.

As a child I used to sit in church listening to talk of God as a being who not only always will be but who always was. Negative infinity. In math class I would get distracted, pondering it. In the West, the organization of reality proceeds from left to right. Out of nothing through the origin and on to infinity. Eventually I figured out that the origin is only where we stand right now. All the same, that zero point on the graph could pull me right down into the rabbit hole. I was okay, somehow, with the up, down, and right-hand lines all stretching off into infinity and the quadrants on the right in their full dimensions doing the same. The left, negative infinity, with its implications of negative time, what did that mean?

The beforehere, the beforewhen.

Lose a baby and you are shoving the child back. Back past the womb, past the heart, past the gleam in your eye. Back beyond the zero on the Cartesian graph.

Look at me, pregnant, doing yoga shoulder stands and skiing four miles per day. See me curled around my growing belly in a papasan chair, reading William Faulkner's collected stories aloud to my un-born son. Now here I am, with a child who is outside me. Here he is, pierced with a dozen needles, being tucked into a life support box for shipment from Boulder to Denver for diagnosis. I am allowed to stroke his arm. Eyes, which have been screwed shut, snap open. He *frowns* at me. Who is sworn to protect him. Sworn, because I'd said, in my heart and out loud, again, again, almost daily for nine months, that I would. When he was two weeks late, I'd become very strident with those promises. Come out, little baby, I'd said. It's safe out here. I will always protect you.

This is a stupid thing for any parent to say. I learned that on the day he was born. I also learned it over time, raising my second son. There is very little a parent can do to protect a child.

I am only on the edge of that lesson now, contemplating him as he lies in this red box being prepared for transport. This box, these nee-dles, this tube down his throat, this is not what we had talked about on all those walks together.

Negative infinity. This child whose soul has appeared from that lower left quadrant on the graph, negative space and time, entered my womb and my mind. Now here before me, eyes boring into mine with full recognition. We have always known one another.

I do get it now.

Pick a point of origin and the graph extends in all directions. It has always existed.

Jacob had the Darsie nose, a legacy from his father. Not just my hus-band's nose, which was quite prominent, but his grandfather's nose, jutting out of photographs on my mother-in-law's wall. Obtrusive and long. "A Roman nose," she would insist. Who knows, given the mix of ethnicity that became Scotland post- all the invasions, including the

Norman one. She may have been right.

Jake's face was shaped around the nose. High forehead, strong cheekbones, none of the facial blurriness often seen in children fresh out of the pelvis. You can't know for sure how a baby will turn out physically, let alone emotionally, or spiritually, as I would discover over the next quarter century with Jacob's younger brother. Still, there were some things about Julian, my subsequent and surviving son, that stayed true, over many years, to my sense of him in the womb and during the early months. I knew Julian was musical, sensitive to the natural world, had an affinity with both his feminine and masculine sides. I couldn't wait to raise him. He too had "the nose," but a broader version of it, to suit a head more square. More like his father's, his grandmother's. After he was born, Julian, like Jacob, had a stillness, a deep-eyed stare that seemed to penetrate those who came to know him.

I want to point to these still-recognizable characteristics in my living son, to say, See? A mother's intuition.

Jake felt, during the pregnancy, like a prophet. Certain and demanding. Charismatic. All parents think their kids are special, but I assure you, *he really was*. A difficult person, perhaps, someone with a hard energy, driven. I was sure I was the right mother for this being.

A half-formed heart didn't fit, symbolically or in any other way. He hadn't seemed at all half-hearted to me. I couldn't believe my baby wasn't strong enough to draw milk from my engorged breasts. Still, he liked to hang out underneath the nipples, reaching up with his lips for a drop, then swishing it around in his mouth. As if to say: Yes, 1989 is a very good year for breast milk.

His vision seemed focused during those few days of his life. Not supposed to be possible. Everyone—the doctors, nurses, the few visitors we allowed—insisted they hadn't seen anything like it. The books said this didn't happen for a couple of weeks at the earliest. His eyes followed us as we moved around. He would arch his back to keep track of his father. It felt as though Jake sensed his time was short, grabbed as much life as he could. Despite his growing weakness, his long, thin arms reached for us, his fingers stroked cheeks, hair. While it was impossible to be sure—sure enough to convince anyone who wasn't there—these gestures did seem intentional, controlled, at least to the extent that he could make his muscles do what he wanted them to do.

Intent. In some non-Western traditions babies are held to be holy beings, having recently arrived from the Divine, the font of creation. They come to us knowing *everything*. We treat them as if they are idiots. They've spent months in the womb listening to and learning our language. It is only in encountering a soulless society or the reality of surviving in harsh conditions that their understanding of who and what they are dulls as the first few months or years pass by.

I myself had not considered this at the time. I thought we had no way to explain to Jake what was going on.

At 25, I was young to face motherhood, at least in my demographic. On the plus side, I was healthy, strong, and so balanced from a daily hatha yoga practice (this was before all the hot yogas and other more aggressive styles came into vogue) that I could water plants from the top of a ladder at seven months pregnant, leaning out on one leg. At about seven and half months, I switched from skis to snowshoes because the baby dropped his head into my pelvis. I felt invincible out there in the snow, smashing tank-like amid the trees. I volunteered one shift per week behind our natural food co-op counter, which meant that most of the town—it was a natural-food kind of town—got to know me through my pregnancy. The local family doctor asked how things were going, and I said, Well, he's dropped, six weeks before my due date.

The doctor said, I heard a joke about precocity one time. The comedian goes, do you realize that by the time Mozart was my age he'd been *dead* for three years?

I did think he was precocious. *He*, not because I'd had an ultrasound—we'd only had that initial screen, when it was too early to tell—but because I simply knew he was a boy. I already thought of him as Jake. In dreams, he was always a boy. Or a young man. Long-haired, loose-limbed, striding along the Continental Divide with a long wooden staff. Going on about physics and literature.

Eavan Boland writes that during a pregnancy, "My mother turned to me. She said/surely you don't believe/you're two souls at this moment?" I *did* think so. The intimacy of housing another body and soul inside your own body and soul is indescribable. But although we were profoundly connected, I knew in the cases of both of my boys that they were themselves.

Making them a full-time job. Each time. I try to do my jobs well. I paid attention and applied myself.

As a kid I often wandered in the cemetery in our New England village, entranced by the stories on the stones. There were whole families buried together, children lined up under mini marble headstones. Dead within a week of one another. Five in this family, seven in that. A couple of rows for this epidemic, a few more for that. Eunice, Jefferson, Innie, Emmaline, Olive, Kittie, Sarah, John, Elmer, Melvin, Mary Ann, Nellie, Walter, Josiah, Martha, Mina, Lucine, Mary Belle, Carrie Jane. The graves of the unnamed babies: "Infant." Worn marble chip after worn marble chip, some impossible to read. Smudges of God's eraser.

The parents must have got used to it. We tell ourselves. Surely, they must.

In 1842 New England's poet lost his son to scarlet fever. "This is lordly man's downlying," he wrote, after his five-year-old son fell to that then-common malady. "Star by star his world resigning."

A threnody is a poem which rages and grieves for its first half. In the second section there's an attempt to make peace with God. Ralph Waldo Emerson's "Threnody" travels as far from faith and into despair as ever the man himself did. Only years later was he able to pick up the poem and finish it. The path to peace for him was in seeing that death defines life. That you wouldn't want to "nail the wild star to the track/ on the half-climbed zodiac" or keep the life force "too starkly pent/in figure, bone, and lineament."

Light is light which radiates
Blood is blood which circulates
Life is life which generates
And many-seeming life is one
Wilt thou transfix and make it none?

Wilt thou? My husband and I were asked this question, as are so many of us now, in so many contexts, for ourselves and for others, when Jacob was born with half his heart missing. At that time, high-resolution ultrasounds at eighteen or twenty weeks were not routinely performed. I was healthy, aware of how to manage a pregnancy; there was no reason to suspect a problem with the pregnancy or the baby. There was no indication of trouble, if you discount, as I do not, a strange nightmare around twenty weeks, or the fact that he was overdue when everything else about him was ahead of schedule. No indication until shortly after the birth, when the pediatrician heard a heart murmur serious enough to send Jacob from our hospital in Boulder to University Hospital in Denver. Even then we were reassured, given the list of heart problems that were "minor," or easily fixed, mostly "down the road." There were three, however, they didn't tell us about until they had to.

Three, invariably fatal.

Three, for which only experimental surgeries were available. Or transplants, which at that time were also experimental. The latest experiment, we were told, had been a baboon heart transplanted into a baby girl called, for the media, "Fae."

The pediatrician knelt at my bedside. He said our son had one of those three conditions. He said, "He is not going to be able to live."

If we were to attempt one of the "heroic" measures to save him, we would have to decide in a matter of hours.

Wilt thou?

Jacob, we tried to absorb, had hypoplastic left heart syndrome, a condition in which, to varying degrees, the left side of the heart does not develop. The left ventricle, one of the heart's four chambers, is the primary pump—it sends oxygenated blood from the lungs back throughout the body, via the aortic artery. The weaker right side of the heart sends blue, oxygen-spent blood to the lungs, a short distance. When the left side is hypoplastic, it may simply have a smaller ventricle. The left ventricular valve may be blocked or may have never formed. The valve opening to the aorta may be undeveloped. In some less-severe cases, surgeons can punch a hole in the atrophied tissue or insert an artificial valve, or one from a pig. There have been recent attempts to perform these operations *in utero*. In more serious cases the tissue surrounding the ventricle is too frozen—lacking plasticity—to pump, or the ventricle is so small it's useless. Sometimes it's not there at all. If the ventricle is not there, it's not there.

HLHS is not detectable in early ultrasounds or in normal neonatal heartbeat monitoring because *in utero* the heart's left side is dormant. The fetus gets its oxygen from the placenta; the left-side pump isn't needed until after birth. In the early days after a child is born, a small shunt sends a mix of oxygenated and unoxygenated blood from the heart to the aorta, the primary artery leaving the heart. As the baby breathes in oxygen with increasing efficiency, and as the left side of the heart expands and figures out its role, the shunt shuts down. In rare cases, this may take weeks, but usually it takes a couple of days. When it closes, babies with HLHS die.

It was just as well no late ultrasound had been performed, I decided later. The pregnancy would have been an entirely different experience had I known I was carrying a child who could not live. Who might indeed have been at least as gifted, intellectually and artistically, as I suspected, but who, for no good reason at all, was doomed. One or two key cells divided wrong, didn't carry the right information, or something, at some point early—the heart being the first organ to form, unless you count blood itself—in the pregnancy. Because of this insultingly random event, the beautiful boy I'd spent so much time and attention building would drown in the blood backing up in his lungs.

In Western culture we still want to believe in miracles. Certain kinds. Not the Madonna on the piece of toast, certainly. Not transubstantiation, literally. Not the survival of Bigfoot, even figuratively (though part of me is still hoping). Instead, we mostly believe that certain miracles can be *worked*, that the people who work them are usually scientists and doctors. People smarter than we are. Sometimes miracles are worked by technology itself. That almost no one dies of scarlet fever anymore is miraculous. On some level we recognize that the gap between the everyday and the miraculous is a function of our own ignorance. That what can seem magical is only the difference between what skilled engineers know and what laypeople don't. There is no divine vestiture, surely, in scientists or doctors, though a book profiling pediatric heart surgeons *is* entitled *Walk on Water*. We call something a miracle if it's something we'd previously failed to imagine.

If it works.

If there is no miracle, we experience something incomprehensible. We don't know how invested we are in the miraculous until there is no such thing available.

I was young to be a mom—most of my pregnant friends were in their thirties at least—but I'd been married young as well, which also was kind of radical among people I'd gone to school with. I won't go into what a mistake that was. A large percentage[1] of couples who lose a child eventually divorce, but I don't think that was our problem. It may be enough to observe that we were one of those pairs who did all right as long as we spent most of the day apart, doing our separate things, coming together in the evenings and on vacations to take part in activities we enjoyed. Parenting required working together in ways we couldn't have anticipated, despite our earnest plans and discussions. The fact that Jake died, and the fact that we loved him so much and were able to decide together what to do—the fact that we agreed on what to do—perpetuated too long the myth of ourselves as well-suited to one another, as well-synched parents.

Before Jake's birth, we had already discussed heroic medicine. Regarding ourselves, our family members, our potential children. We hadn't exactly discussed *babies*. We didn't bother with a television in the remote valley where we lived, but we read the paper, we'd heard of children on life support, we thought we wouldn't keep parents or relatives alive past their time, we wouldn't want that for ourselves. I'd had a horse wreck where I'd thought I might be killed. It had taken me two years to be able to tilt my head backward, to be able to read for more than twenty minutes at a time, and though I had no diagnosis, in a few years' more time I would come to understand I'd probably suffered a mild brain injury. It took decades to find myself fully recovered from that. If I am. I think I am.

---

[1] The statistic we were given at the time by the medical professionals and later in our grief group was that 80 percent of marriages with lost children fail; this did not seem accurate based on simple observation of the bereaved parents we knew. Nowadays the number cited is 28 percent. This awkwardness—stats we were cited at the time of our decision—or that my memory produces for me—vs. what is known now—persists throughout this essay. Even the more current figures seem to change often.

Not even a year after that event, my husband had been in a head-on collision with a drunk driver while traveling home from work. He too had nearly died and wasn't fully recovered. When you're young, you plow through things. We had no idea we were still injured; no one had told us. It is only because we healed over time—over *years*— that we could see how damaged we'd been previously. Even then, the impacts from these physical traumas and from the catastrophe of our son's death would be hard to separate.

Because of these accidents, we at least understood we were not immortal. Unlike many of our peers, we never questioned the need for medical insurance. My husband was a subcontractor who didn't have benefits; we paid for Kaiser out of pocket, though of course it was cheaper then. In our mid-twenties, we already had living wills, surprisingly rare even today among my now much older friends.

After they penetrated Jacob with a dozen needles, they forced a tube down his throat. We understood the violence of this all too well. When my husband's car was hit by the drunk driver's car, he was not wearing his seat belt. Because the engine was shoved into the driver's compartment, this failure might have saved his life. Or at least his legs. On the other hand, not wearing a seatbelt also nearly killed him. He was driving a convertible with the top down. He was thrown forward such that his throat hit the top of the windshield, crushing his windpipe. Intubation saved his life. When he awakened in the ICU, drugged to the gills, all he wanted to do was rip the tube from his throat.

We watched, horrified, as our newborn endured what we knew was an agonizing introduction to the world. The glass box was buckled shut. Jake was heaved into an ambulance. I was escorted back to my bed to recover from the drugs my birth plan had clearly stated I didn't want administered.

Almost anything, they told us, could be fixed these days. It's amazing, we realized later, what is thought of as easily fixed. Same with "life support." The torture box I just described. "Life support," as if it were a miracle, not a hell for the person inside. Easily fixed: heart surgeries, to repair holes, or misfiring valves in hearts the size of grapes. Hearts in the sawn-open chests of infants.

I lay there in tears, listening to babies crying in other rooms while their mothers learned to soothe them. I waited to hear which "easily fixed" condition our son would have. Around noon the pediatrician entered the room and I saw his face. My husband was right behind him, and I saw *his* face.

The pediatrician did not think there were any real miracles on offer for our son. But we did have a decision to make. We had three choices.

Option A: Transplant. Neonatal cadaver hearts were and still are rare, tiny organs nearly impossible to find. Today, about a fifth[2] of babies with fatal defects die while waiting for a heart. The average wait is one year, with some form of mechanical support required in the meantime. The more urgent the need, the more likely the child is to die before receiving a heart. Yet the younger the child, the better the chances of long-term survival, because the infant's immune system is less developed, less likely to fight off the invading organ. Back in 1989, none of this was known. That a younger baby might have more success was only conjecture. The only example our doctors were able to cite was the unsuccessful baboon heart transplant, though it turned out that there had been a few other baby heart transplants already. The only transplant center for babies was in L.A., we were told. We lived in the mountains outside Boulder. The geography was not a dealbreaker in and of itself, but something else to give us pause, considering the unlikelihood of finding a heart. Not to mention the murky picture regarding long-term survival, for which there were no statistics available then, either.

Option B: Surgery. A procedure, or rather a sequence of three procedures over a couple of years if he survived each stage. The idea was to replumb the system so the right side of the heart could function as both a receptacle for the unoxygenated blood coming in from the venous system and as a pump for the arterial blood returned from the lungs. We were told there was a 50 percent survival rate for the first phase only. Survival meant only that they came out of surgery alive and lived for an unspecified duration after. Our doctors believed that the chances would not improve with the successive phases. Again, no long-term data were available, and because no one knew how well a

---

[2] I have also seen one-third, and two-thirds.

one-sided heart could carry a person into adulthood, a transplant was considered likely down the road. I don't think we knew this at the time, but another HLHS parent, Amy Kuebelbeck, author of *Waiting with Gabriel*, told us some years later that most transplants failed after 8-12 years. Her son was diagnosed 20 weeks into her pregnancy, so she'd had lots (by our lights) of time to research. In adults today, a heart transplant buys about a decade of life. So, with the best outcome, Jake would need a new heart again. Again.

We were told the first phase of the surgery was performed in only one place at that time: Philadelphia, another geographical challenge for us, located as we were in the center of America. Now there are other transplant and surgery centers, including Denver.

Jacob did not seem very stable on life support. Our doctors wondered if he would live long enough to get a heart or would qualify for surgery.

If we "selected" either "option"— transplant or surgery—we would have to move, possibly for months. You could see the conflict of interest fluttering in the face of our Kaiser Permanente pediatrician, whom we really did like, as he told us what the choices might cost: upwards of $100,000 (a bargain, compared to today), and his uncertainty over whether Kaiser would cover it. (The hell you won't, I thought. I might seem bloated, unwashed, young, and clobbered, but I will turn this into a PR nightmare for Kaiser.) The cardiologist and the pediatrician both told us that they had no way of knowing without being in that position themselves, but they thought that if it were their kid, they would find the decision very hard to make. They did not have much confidence in the medical options and felt a lot of suffering would be involved. They hoped, personally, that they would have the courage not to pursue either of the "miraculous" options.

So, Option C: Comfort care. Hold him and love him for every second of his life. Allow him to die in our arms instead of inside of a box.

We had only hours to decide. The internet was a primitive thing then. Calling the two centers, trying to find parents who had children further along in the processes, felt overwhelming. Instead, we trusted our instincts.

Such as they were.

Intuition again. I believed, as Emerson did, that my child could save the world. I know many mothers believe something along these lines of their children, especially now, when parents are having their kids so much later in their lives, when they've had a chance themselves to acquire advanced degrees and become quite accomplished in their careers. Now, parents have high expectations for everything. Back then this wasn't so much the case. As I said, I was younger than most of the other mothers I knew. But even the "old" mothers were only in their early or mid-thirties. Many of my friends worked part-time or did not work outside the home because we were mostly post-hippies, or at least vegetarians. We leaned toward Montessori or Waldorf. The kids wore organic cotton clothing, were breastfed in public (I was only vaguely aware there was a controversy about this), played with wooden toys. They climbed trees unsupervised, were dragged in sleds behind cross-country skis, were treated for minor ailments with herbal remedies rather than rushed to the emergency room for every little ear infection. That is, we were thoughtful and attachment-oriented, but this wave of parenting was before the helicopter thing.

So, most mothers believe their children are special. My support for my own belief came from having done nothing during my pregnancy other than turn inward, feel into the experience, feel into *him*. Pay attention to my dreams, the rhythm of my child's sleep/wake cycles, the patterns of his movements. I wrote, walked in the woods, read aloud to my baby, did yoga daily, napped when I felt tired. Those months were filled with practices that honed intuition. I didn't feel guilty about the fact that I wasn't "working." I was writing a novel, or learning how to. I was incarnating a human soul.

The fact that I stayed home put a lot of strain on our finances and marriage. We lived for years with plywood floors, an avocado-colored fridge, crappy wiring. We heated our ongoing remodeling project with wood, fighting steady winter winds of at least sixty miles per hour that gusted up to a hundred. Our home, in a mountain ghost-town/summer-home assembly of cabins, many of which still had Old-West style storefronts, was on the alpine/sub-alpine transition zone. Whatever was happening atop the Continental Divide was happening on our roof, though just a mile down-valley things might be balmier. It could blizzard well into June, or as early as September. Lilacs didn't blossom till early July. Life scarcely seemed easy, but I loved the elemental feel of our lives just below treeline, how gossip with our neighbors was more likely to be about mountain lion behavior and the wind than to be about each other.

I'd made a deal with my husband. I had a mood imbalance I didn't then have a name for. I just knew something was "wrong." Staying stable took a lot of daily management in the form of exercise, yoga, healthy eating. Important for everyone; an ironclad necessity for me. Because of all that careful self-care and the lack of external stress from college or work, I'd had a relatively long period of stability. I understood I wouldn't be able to work full-time and be a good mom and a writer. I thought I could do two out of three. My husband had agreed to be the breadwinner while I stayed home with any children and wrote.

It seemed we'd made sound choices, especially for our ages.

We were well on our way to building a good life.

If I'd sinned, I suppose it was in feeling smug about that.

In my defense, I would say I was too young to know any better.

Intuition: who do you feel your newborn or unborn child is? The kind of life our doctors were outlining, even with the best outcomes, even with hoped-for improvements in anti-rejection protocols, meant multiple surgeries through the breastbone. This kind of thing takes a very patient child.

In *The Black Hole War*, theoretical physicist Leonard Susskind shares an anecdote of walking with Stephen Hawking and some others in San Francisco. No sooner had they crested one of the city's famous hills when Hawking hit the juice in his wheelchair, schussing down the street. Much to the dismay of his companions.

"Stephen Hawking, daredevil!" Susskind exclaims.

Hawking found, one assumes, a satisfying life of the mind combined with stealth grabs for adrenaline. Maybe a similar balance would have worked for Jake. It's not impossible. To me, though, it felt unlikely. I thought he would rail against the finite.

I thought he would resent the life of a lab rat, his suffering dedicated to medical knowledge, to the saving or extension of the lives of other, future children.

Perhaps I might have made a different decision for a different child. Not necessarily a personality with less steam or reach, or even drive, but possibly more willingness to accept the universe as it is or as it appears to be. Perhaps in that case I would have just "known" what to do, perhaps then I might have judged others who "knew" differently. A schoolmate rants regularly on Facebook about parents who have not chosen to go to the same extremes he and his family have pursued to fight a rare, vicious, and nearly always fatal form of childhood cancer. Perhaps if his particular son were mine, I would do what he has been doing. Or what the writer Aleksandr Hemon describes having done for his baby daughter, who also suffered from that cancer. These are parents who do "everything."

Here I am, again. Bringing up a fuzzy term like "intuition," when it's so unnecessary. Any rational person can see that the numbers are not good, for stage-four rhabdo, or for HLHS.

Irrationally, had we gone for a transplant, we would have been called brave. Pioneers. Fighters. No question that we were doing everything that could be done. *Life* magazine might have featured us, instead of, as it did not long after Jake's death, a mother who refused to pick up her baby while he awaited a transplant. She said she was afraid he would die in her arms.

We were afraid Jake would die when we *weren't* holding him.

To put our child through what our doctors and nurses were describing because we couldn't face his death. To get ourselves off the hook by stringing him to wires and tubes. To let our own fear of death rule his life. That would be selfish of us, we thought.

It is wrong for a child to die. Always wrong. Nonetheless, Nature fails, and children do die.

We choose among least-worst outcomes throughout our lives. They're out of Klondike ice cream bars at the store, and nothing really compares, does it? Moving from a neighborhood you love to one you don't, for the sake of a school. The college your child wants to attend but that would send you deeply into debt, versus the state school you can afford.

Making a decision regarding a child's life before they can even communicate is an extreme example. Abortion may well be the closest comparison. Some women face the possibility of bearing a child at the wrong time in their lives—wrong for whatever reasons, including never wanting children—or with a man who is dangerous or just worthless as a father, or bearing a child with serious internal "defects" that mean the child will live in agony after birth. Ending such a pregnancy can mean severing a connection with a soul that may have already begun speaking to them in dreams, in tastebuds, in their apprehension of the world.

While pregnant with my second child I had to have two fetal echocardiograms (super high-resolution ultrasounds focused on the heart) at around 16- and 20-weeks' gestation. It was nearly impossible to sleep during that waiting period. I think my husband's sleep cycles were permanently destroyed. As for me, I'd already felt Julian move—and with an early pattern very different from his brother's. I'd been in contact with his soul. What if the tests were positive? Would I carry him through the pregnancy and repeat our horrific experience? Or abort, never having had the chance to look him in the eye?

Negative against negative and despite the mathematical and grammatical laws, no positive outcome. Or at least no decision leading to the place you want to get.

Luckily, miraculously, the echo too was negative. Our second son's heart was fully formed.

If you lose a child when he is young, it is likely you are also young. So much of your life is still to live, so much of yourself is still to be found. Now, already, your life has forked irretrievably. Much of who you might have become is lost, while a new self, built or warped to confront questions that might never otherwise have arisen, will be wrought.

This is weird.

You may find yourself grateful for the changes while at the same time feeling enraged. You wouldn't want to be the blithe idiot you, by definition now, were before. But you would never, ever want to have had to go through this, and you never, ever wanted your child to die.

One thing no one tells you, not even in the grief books, which almost never speak of what happens to you over the course of decades, is that over some serious time, you will begin to contemplate matters from angles you might never have anticipated. If you lost a child when you were *very* young, then maybe you have never lost *anyone* before. Maybe it will take a while before you lose anyone again. Maybe it will be some time before you start going to other funerals, before you have other people to talk to about death. About rituals. About souls and where they go. Maybe, over time, your own beliefs will change. Maybe you will begin to feel that you might have done things wrong.

Even if you were smart and read all the books, wrote in your journal and went to grief groups, tried to be prepared, and—

You were just so young.

Suddenly. Overnight. We were not going to be raising the child I knew. Our lives were not going to have the shape we envisioned. I was not going to be the mother I had believed in. Who were we going to be?

"I have no reference points for this," I said to a nurse.

We didn't belong to a church. My spiritual beliefs were only in the process of forming. I was doing at least an hour of yoga daily, at a time when yoga teachers usually had been to India several times, maybe having lived there for many years. I spent so much time in the woods. My dreams were intense. Some of them seemed to convey a fuller knowledge of my surroundings than I could have obtained in waking life. For instance, our local ski area had been closed for years. Even when it re-opened, the steep back bowl, exposed to high winds, remained shut. I had a fun dream of skiing down the back side and through the woods to our home. During my pregnancy with Jake, a blizzard laid down enough snow for the area's new owners to open the back runs. I was an expert skier; I'd been doing one-legged yoga poses for years and had excellent balance. There was no way I wasn't going to ski those black runs. Sure enough, the terrain, not visible from the hiking trails I used below, was identical to what I saw in my dream.

I also dreamed repeatedly of thunderbirds. Upon attending a lecture by a neighbor on the prehistory of the valley, I learned that members of the Arapaho and Cheyenne tribes had told him the thunderbird made its home in our section of mountains. He said these tribes used to take youths who were scared of lightning to the high lakes above our valley for initiations. Another neighbor had been doing archaeological excavations at these lakes and confirmed their importance in vision quests.

I found all this interesting, but unactionable. It made me a little more confident in my intuition. It affirmed my connection to the landscape. Some Native American literature I read around this time suggested that visions were embedded in the land. One late-twentieth century Lakota man reported seeing a band of 19th century Indians riding horseback, only to fade away into the tall grasses, as if he were viewing a memory belonging to the earth itself. The bond I was forming with my valley seemed nearly as intense as the one I was building with my child. I think perhaps this bond would have led me to beliefs that were very rich, if my son had not died. If, just as I was beginning to recover spiritually, my marriage had not begun to die, if divorce and the need to earn my own living had not forced me out of the valley.

Reference points: Jake's father and I had only been living in our little ghost town for a couple of years. Having left our families of origin years before, we were 2,000 miles from where we'd grown up. If we moved to either center of surgery, we would be far from anyone we knew and far from my husband's means of supporting us. Thanks to an insurance settlement from my husband's accident, we had planned for him to quit his hated job, to bond as a family for about another month while he researched small businesses he might develop, perhaps home-based. Then we would invest the rest of the settlement in whichever venture he chose. That was it, that was all we had thought of. We had no other gear to shift into.

Neither one of us was the type to change plans easily. It would not have occurred to us to say, Oh, we can mortgage or sell the house we have just bought, in which we have a fair amount of equity (thanks, again, to the insurance settlement). I had just turned 26. My husband was 28. We were still accustomed to just scraping by as college students. We didn't think in terms of our strengths. Nor did we have anyone we could ask. No relative or older friend offered any advice or asked us any questions about our assets. No one said, I bet you guys can't think for shit right now, here are some approaches you might not have considered.

We might have found a way to afford the surgery and the moves. But it was not about the money, anyway.

Before we'd moved to the mountains and I'd begun a long writing project, before my head injury, I'd majored in International Affairs and Soviet Studies, writing my honors thesis on Afghanistan. I'd planned at one point to go to grad school to study the ways great powers manipulated ethnic groups in countries bordering rival states. I'd thought a lot about how groups were set against each other and how permanent warfare could ensue. How in some regions foreigners were just never accepted. How these policies usually backfired on the countries promulgating them. The body is programmed to reject outsiders. Once you transplant an organ, I thought, you Balkanized the body.

"Major organ failure—that's what death *is*," I said to a nurse.

We saw either medical path as ultimately leading to a transplant, and Jacob's resulting life as a trenched battle that would never end, a battle we would be drafting our son into whether he liked it or not. Some people would see this as engaging in a heroic struggle for life. Instead, we saw it as forcing our son to spend his whole life fighting *not* to die.

In a poetry reading series I frequently attend, the moderator usually asks the featured poets to name their worst fear. Losing my second child, now an adult, is my worst fear. Losing my husband, statistically likely to die before me, is another horrific thought. This isn't what the moderator is after. She wants to know about spiders, snakes, monsters under the bed. Things you don't admit. My secret worst fear would be black holes. They do wander around. We could cross paths with one. If you somehow fell into a black hole, of course you would be crushed instantly. Except it wouldn't seem instant to you. Anyone watching you approach the event horizon would see you fly into it and vanish, crushed or dissolved at very near the speed of light. However, the experience of time is relative. Time dilates at the event horizon. So, to you, your agonizing dismemberment would be virtually eternal.

There is no time in the womb. The child is eternally present with its mother during gestation. What happens to the baby, pleasant or unpleasant, including during birth, marks it forever, those who specialize in birth trauma have said. The resolution of birth trauma is not exactly mainstream, but now it's widely argued among child development experts—see, for instance, *Born Anxious* by Daniel Keating—that *conception* to age one is the key period in human development. I really cannot see how we can dismiss the possibility of birth trauma extending far into a person's life. Because the infant cannot keep time, it cannot discern beginnings and endings. Even well into adulthood, some part of us may not be able to recognize that the threat—a cord wrapped around our neck, an emergency c-section causing our mother to panic, birthing teams who do not know how to ease the transition into the world of bright light and unfiltered noise—ever passed. This is what happens with PTSD as well. Time dilates during the stressful experience, and to the PTSD sufferer, the experience is always there, in an eternal now. Keating was talking about how the mother's circumstances—poverty, an abusive or insecure relationship, a high-powered, demanding job—affect her brain wiring. That chemistry in turn builds the child's wiring in some cases, leading it to be born anxious. I would push harder on this. Other factors, external ones, occurring during this time of no-time, which might extend well into the first year, could conceivably be experienced as eternal truths.

If you died, for instance, in agony. Over what looked to others like days or hours.

To those who knew your parents or who read your mother's writing, it may seem as if you lived and died in only three and half days, an instant. Your parents underwent this trauma with you, and yet apart from you. This was your first lesson of living, your apartness, and you hadn't even begun to process it. Now you are dying, apart. Your heart imploding in its effort to drag oxygen out of your bloodied lungs. Possibly eternally. Your parents know more about time. They know your death came to an end. But for them, too, time dilated. You have fallen into the hole. They spin around it, just outside the horizon, caught by the gravity well.

Bearing children, of course, comes with any number of risks. Somewhere along the way, in a pregnancy book, or whispered from friend to friend, family to family, you learn of them. They are in the very back of your mind. In college I worked as an aide on a school bus for extremely disabled kids. I saw what the parents of children with severe autism, spina bifida, chromosomal disorders, cerebral palsy, microcephaly, coped with. When I was three or four, my cousin Aaron had died of SIDS. When I was five, a boy I played with died of pneumonia. In our childbirth class, a couple mentioned that their first baby had been stillborn. Theoretically, things can go wrong.

Theoretically, I could die in a car crash. I could die riding a horse. I rock climb, and I ski in avalanche terrain, though in both cases I do everything I can to minimize the risks. Certainly, friends of friends— even very careful people—have been killed in those pursuits. Theoretically, I could have borne an unhealthy child, or had a placental abruption or a cord accident. But the likelihood seemed remote. More than just being young and strong, I was, I felt, a good *person*. I'd worked hard in school. I'd worked hard to put myself through school. I was a good neighbor and involved in my community. I was *smart*. I *recycled*. I bought *dolphin-safe tuna*. Nearly every day I communed with my surroundings. I say with utter certainty that there was never a day I lived in the Eldora Valley when I wasn't awestruck by its beauty, when my heart didn't open to those mountains as I came around the last corner toward home. Every day I felt lucky, grateful. Whyever would Nature sabotage *me?*

Sure, you take a risk just breathing the air of this world. There is simply no way to make yourself more vulnerable than to bring your own offspring into the world. But that's an emotional and spiritual risk. The risk of death, the risk to your health and to the child—well, of course it's *there*. But it's not exactly like going to the casino. It's not like the deck is stacked. It's not like you're an *idiot* for playing. You know, vaguely, that there's some risk, and that someone is going to pay. But it is not going to be you.

Emerson's child: "born for the future, to the future lost." This sums up what any grief book will tell you about losing a child. You lose not just the person, but the dream, the future. What the world would have been with him in it. Emerson wrote that so much of his grief for his son came from the loss of that general hope, from outrage that a child who "should ills of ages" have stayed would be taken by a fleeting illness. Wasn't there a single angel, he wondered, who could stoop "to save that only child?"

And, truly, who would *not* want to fight such a fate? It *is* a miracle of modern medicine that we've reduced epidemics affecting our children to the ones we choose. Hunger and war.

Imagine the numbness in those households only a century ago, imagine the prostration, the stars resigned. So, I suppose we carry with us an echo of these nightmares when we fight to save our children, or even to hold on to our own lives, to our parents' lives. When we do what it takes to give the lie to that prayer so many of us grew up saying before bed: "If I should die before I wake, I pray the Lord my soul to take."

Didn't we lie awake in terror after reciting that?

No, no, no. We don't want death to be arbitrary.

It *is*, though.

No matter how we try to get out of dying, no matter how much the miracle workers try to prolong our lives, the fact remains that we don't get to pick when or how we go. This inability to control our end seems to be part of the contract. We can cheat here and there, but there's something discomfiting about that. A deal with the devil, in which our death may turn out worse than if we'd just gone quietly in the first place. Whether it's round four of chemotherapy or outlandish surgery, we merely trade in one date we couldn't pick for another date we won't be able to pick. With possibly worse circumstances.

We might, as many science fiction writers fervently hope will happen, unlock the secret of aging, somehow making eternal or extremely prolonged life available to everyone. But I believe we will tire of it. One reason is that some of us will still die. Some diseases will persist, or new ones will arise. People will murder. Others will be traumatized, live miserably—they will commit suicide for one reason or another. Still others will die in accidents. That is, we will *miss* one another. At some point we will long to know what happened to them; we will resign our stars, longing to follow our loved ones unto death, just to see.

I'm shocked at how far we have not come in our conversation about death and dying since 1989. In the early 90s, I taught several sections of a college composition and rhetoric course around the story of Karen Ann Quinlan, who was famously brain dead. Students had to analyze the arguments for and against letting her die. Almost all the kids were in favor of letting her go. People were signing living wills and discussing Do Not Resuscitate orders.

Yet today, many of my friends fight to keep their 90+ terminally ill parents alive, even when they are unconscious, then write blogs or memoirs about the shock of loss. How, I wonder, having lost a child, is the death of parents shocking? Friends, a married couple in their late sixties, recently asked me if I had a living will. They were surprised to learn that I'd had one since my twenties. They had only begun to discuss this matter between themselves.

Last winter I stopped to talk with a neighbor, a former professor of poetry, as I walked my dog. I asked how his wife was doing after back surgery; he told me about her deteriorating vision and hearing. Everyone thinks it's great that we're living so long, he said. No one realizes how depressed many of us are. These impacts of aging don't apply to everyone, but when I mention these possibilities to others my own age or younger, they shake their heads and insist that it is all a matter of healthy living. As if kale will somehow prevent nerve deafness.

Not long ago, *Psychology Today* carried an article exploring the lives of four people living with advanced cancer. New treatments had made it possible for them to continue to live normally despite metastasized tumors that otherwise would have been death sentences. One, in his sixties, had recently fathered a child. A survivor in her seventies complained of the difficulty of constantly managing her fear of death. And I thought, Who do you think you are? My very fit father dropped dead of a heart attack at 73. Who was this woman to complain that her high-tech cancer treatment still leaves her under the shadow of death? To feel entitled to freedom from the fact of death? At any time, let alone in her seventies?

This reflexive fear of death. This turning of our faces from dying, and from our fear. Isn't it what drives so much of everything that's wrong with our world? Isn't this exactly what we need to examine, on both ends of life, even in the middle? If there's a beforehere, and I'm convinced of that, an afterhere seems possible. I don't even care what it is. Surely our short time on earth, that narrow area on the graph between negative and positive infinity, can't be something to cling to. Three days, thirty years, three hundred years—these lifespans are the same in the face of eternity. We all die. In *Mortality*, Christopher Hitchens, who had no belief in an afterhere at all, argued there is just no *sense* in trying so hard not to.

I don't mean to echo those posts I see on Facebook or in response to online articles about COVID-19, wherein people, or possibly trolls, argue that we're all going to die anyway and there's no sense in upending our economy over it. Aside from the fact that there is every sense in upending the U.S. economy, the pandemic having highlighted all of its weaknesses, I mean that the blind fear that seems to drive us to fight death in almost all circumstances is, like all fear-based behavior, not leading us anywhere good. Perhaps we're missing the point of death.

It took Emerson five years to return to the second portion of his "Threnody" and to begin to respond to the painful questions he'd thrown from the heart of grief to God, Nature, Infinity.

"Deep Heart" answers him. Basically, it says, how else would you have it? Without death?

When frail Nature can no more,
Then the Spirit strikes the hour,
My servant Death, with solving rite,
Pours finite into infinite.
Wilt thou freeze love's tidal flow,
Whose streams through nature circling go?

Transcendentalist Ralph Waldo Emerson was a 19th-century hippie. He was Christian in a woodsy, let's-start-a-commune sort of way. He knew all the cool people—Henry David Thoreau, Louisa May Alcott, Margaret Fuller, Nathaniel Hawthorne, and possibly Emily Dickinson. Emerson came to the conclusion that his son was lost in god (his lowercase), but "in godhead found." Death, while a great source of anguish, was also necessary for the growth of the soul, even for the growth of those left behind. It fueled *life*. Without it, we would stagnate, "conned to tediousness," deceived into believing that "figure, bone, and lineament" were entirely what we were. It is Death, a servant of the divine, that pours "finite into infinite." Moving us into the more mysterious quadrants of the graph. When? When Spirit strikes the hour. Spirit knows when it is time to go.

If we believe in Spirit. I myself turn away from the content of most religious systems, if not from their impulses. I studied comparative religion in graduate school. I am capable of seeing terms like "godhead" and "my servant Death" as products of their contexts, their times and places, as metaphors that can still be useful if one is trained in interpreting these tropes. I really don't mind them. For many, these terms are so loaded, they are simply unacceptable. I don't know what to do about this, because we don't yet have others that don't sound even more ridiculous. Sometimes I just go around calling God the "great woo-woo." Stuff we can't explain. Things I've experienced but am too lazy to put a narrative around, because after all it's the narrative that's gotten so many cultures into trouble. What is not only woo-woo to me but also *great*, skeptics will label wishful thinking or confirmation bias, but, frankly, fuck them. I'll wager none of them have ever been pregnant, or have had encounters with dead children. I would ask them to consider, instead, a version of Pascal's wager: which kind of jerk would you rather be? The kind who doesn't want to be made to feel foolish, suckered out of extreme need into having a little faith, or the kind that might dismiss as superstition an attempted communication from your own dead child? Which mistake is more awful?

I'd rather take the line that death is possibly a "solving rite," instead of a personal apocalypse. What I know is that my son's personhood appeared. Then, when "frail Nature" could no more, it disappeared. That same spirit I'd sensed within my field when Jacob was incarnating, I also sensed leaving as he died. Spirit struck the hour. Too soon, I felt, and too soon, I think, he felt. It was startling and shattering for all of us to learn that Nature would fail so quickly. But keeping the powerful being that I had sensed from so early in the pregnancy tethered to such a frail Nature did not seem like an enterprise that would be successful—

And yet.

Over time, different aspects of losing Jacob have afflicted me. Even now, thirty years later, the cold assails me. What does your mother nag you about, always and forever, to this day, no matter how old you are? It drives you crazy. Put your hat on. Don't forget your gloves. Zip up that coat. You're not going outside in *those* shoes, are you? Would you like an extra blanket? Here, I'll get one, keep it at the foot of your bed, just in case.

Isn't your mother still sending you gloves for Christmas? Isn't she still knitting you scarves and socks? Don't you have piles and piles?

There are any number of culturally proscribed ways for a mother to do ill, in any number of societies. The surest way I know to fail a child is to allow it to become cold.

In every grief memoir written by a mother you will find this: the obsession with the lost child's terrific cold. Her inability to keep him warm. It drives a grieving mother out of her mind. Even when we come back to ourselves, there is something nagging at us forever, some bit of energy we are using, every minute of every day, to close the door on that voice that is constantly telling us about this wrong we have done, this great, irredeemable failure of ours, in addition to all of the other categorical failures involved with allowing a child to die. We have a child who is in the utter dark, in the utter cold. We are not keeping him warm.

This is a horror that has never left me, even as I recognize that by now, he is no longer an infant lost in a cold, dark place. Wherever he is, whatever has become of him, surely he has gone on from that.

Over time, I've come to be horrified by other matters. I am in my late fifties now, and friends of mine have died. Family members have died, and family members of friends have died. Stories have been shared. There have been beautiful deaths, and stories of beautiful death rituals. How it seemed that Mary's room filled up with presences at the end. How, in the weeks before she died, Liz kept dreaming of relatives and friends who had died before her. How Susan's uncle woke from his coma, focused his eyes, and seemed to track an unseen person moving from the doorway to the side of his bed. ("But why do they always come through the *door*?" says my current husband, a widower.) I love these stories and they seem so consistent. Hospice nurses repeat them and have written books about them. If they're wishful thinking, who's harmed? How much worse for us to dismiss them if they're true.

It tortures me that I can think of no one who might have come for my son. Other than my cousin, whom I saw only once, as a very young child, no one—no relative I knew of or friend—had died before him. He went into that night entirely alone.

Worse, we *sent* him into that night entirely alone.

In the weeks and months following Jake's death, we didn't face as much judgment for our decision as we feared. Worse were the dismissive, minimizing comments, meant to reassure the speaker more than us, about our experience. "At least you weren't attached," one person said. "Everything happens for a reason," my mother intones to this day. "You're young, you can have more children," was a common statement. I did what I could to assert Jacob's personhood, publishing an essay accompanied by a half-dozen photographs in the Boulder *Sunday Camera Magazine* about him and about our decision and our loss. My husband and I received an outpouring of letters and phone calls in sympathy and support. Some women wrote that the article had caused them to name an infant lost decades ago, or to endow a scholarship or plant a tree—to otherwise mark a deep wound unacknowledged by family or community. I thought again of the belief that women "back then," when infant loss was common, bore these losses more easily— the women bore them easily, or society did?

Some called us courageous. As the years have gone by, however, my own confidence in this picture of us has been shaken. A little. It's *mostly* true, I think, that we put Jacob first. But it's also a little true that I would have struggled terribly to live alongside Jake in the life he would have required. If he was not a patient child, neither am I a patient woman.

Nor am I stable.

There had always been something a little off about me, according to my mother. I felt it, too. Because of whatever it was, I hadn't intended to have children at all. However, after a few years of living in the mountains recovering from my horse wreck—basically, after some years of no real stress at all—I felt as if that thing that was wrong had left me.

In high school and college, I measured the success of a life—or rather, I measured life—by achievement. When I shared my early career goals, which for a long time seriously included saving the world with my skills in Russian and International Affairs—we were expecting a nuclear holocaust back then—some friends would ask, with a degree of hostility, will that make you *happy*? I was mystified by this question. Why wouldn't you be happy making a difference in the world? Most of all, *what was* this happiness of which everyone seemed to speak? Honestly, I had never experienced it.

After college, as I learned how to take care of myself, found a congenial community, developed another way to express my abilities through writing, I began to get a glimpse. This glimpse grew into a vision and an experience of happiness. I wanted to preserve it. I stayed stable within this experience for three years. With everything so aligned, I thought perhaps I could have a child after all. I had no idea that stability for me, by definition, does not last.

I was at that time engaged in a very sad process of coming to terms with the difference between ability and capability, an uneasy acceptance that has followed me everywhere. In college I told a favorite professor of Eastern European history, the late Stephen Fischer-Galati, that I was afraid of a normal professional career. I couldn't imagine, I said, working 8-5 or even 9-5. Five times per week, four weeks per month. I couldn't figure out why. I was about to graduate *summa cum laude*. My graduate school entrance scores were very high. There was a surfeit of ability. I sensed, though, that having to show up at about the same time, day after day, wasn't in my wiring.

The professor was understanding. This was sometimes the very reason people went into academia, he said. Even if you had to teach an 8 a.m. class, it wasn't every day of the week, and it would likely be for only one semester. There would be plenty of time during vacations, weekends, summers, and even between classes for an *able* person to do work of one's own.

As he talked, I began to think that perhaps becoming a professor might be a job I was *capable* of. Versus: I could go to law school, and be *able* to rock the house down, but was I *capable* of becoming a lawyer, with the straight-on, no-rest schedules, not to mention performance anxiety? Would I be *able* to sleep if I had such a high-stress profession, and if not, would I be *capable* in the field? Already I had understood how important sleep was to my capabilities.

By the time Jake was born, the head injury prior to graduation had affected my capabilities regarding an academic career. Later I did go back to graduate school, and my husband's resentment over my choice affected those capabilities in a different way.

Nearly anyone can have a child. Some people will have exacting standards as to what raising a child will look like. I had already wondered about my capabilities as a mother, given the liabilities of uneven sleep patterns, uneven mood, the need for (a lot of) regular exercise, and other self-care necessities. A friend accused me of being obsessive-compulsive about exercise, which hurt, in the way that being misunderstood by someone close to you always hurts. It wasn't a function of being thin. This was what I *had* to do, in order not to be hated, in order not to be too much for people. My whole life, starting from perhaps the age of five, I'd felt judged for my emotional storms. Though I didn't yet have a name for what those closest to me seemed to feel was wrong with me, I'd found a way to manage my moods. Everyone should exercise, but I needed to be exhausted, physically, mentally, emotionally, every day, in order not to drive those I loved away. Exercise was part of the program. So was doing yoga. And writing. It all took up a lot of time, and in itself, I later came to see, my self-management program was also exhausting for those around me.

Perhaps it just wasn't possible for me to be Jacob's mother, after all. After all those months of utter certainty that I was his ideal parent, perhaps there was a basic incapacity that meant this task was simply too much for me.

During the doctors' explanations of the long but still only partial list of implications involved in choosing "heroic" surgery, a deep fatigue came over me. If I suggest that intuition played a role in our decision, perhaps helping guide us on Jacob's behalf, I must also acknowledge some inner guidance, no matter how unconscious, about *my* needs, my husband's needs, and the burden on our relationship. Maybe that's just as important to take those factors into account, says a friend. It's a system, not a baby in isolation. If you aren't built to raise a severely compromised child, that's part of the truth of the matter.

There's a lot of question these days about the existence of the soul. Sometimes it's hard to believe in it. Terry Eagleton has dubbed the strawperson conceptualization of religion represented in the writings of Richard Dawkins and Christopher Hitchens as the "Ditchkins" approach. With the Ditchkins pseudo-philosophy has arisen what is claimed to be a rationally "skeptical" take on everything that might smack of the hereafter or the beforehere, including the concept of a soul. And as time has passed since my pregnancies and the births of my children, I, facing the increasing numbers of deaths of family members, close friends, even pets, have had more difficulty knowing what I know. Still. There was a time, even a specific moment, when my children's souls were *here*. When they hadn't been here before.

Some will say my experiences are subjective (of course they are; they are experiences). They will suggest that the arrival of the soul is linked to some period of development in the child's brain. (I believe Dawkins claims, without any more evidence than the next mother, this very thing.) That is, a certain level of electrical activity creates a personality, a spirit that will die when the brain stops generating those impulses. It might follow that a woman who is paying attention—a woman such as I, who made building a human a full-time job—will notice when this occurs in the fetus she is carrying. And I suppose you could also argue that an attuned woman may sense the child's developing consciousness, because, after all, fetal cells have been found within a mother's brain years after the child is grown and gone. I am able and willing to argue all of these things.

But honestly, this postulated ability to sense a child's developing consciousness, which in turn is based on electrical signaling, which I regard as not untrue, sounds just as woo-woo as anything else.

So, perhaps. Or perhaps it's just that there's a baseline level of electrical activity required for the soul to fully attach to a fetus. The soul waits till the brain and body are "ready" for it. I had a sense of my children as individuals long before the 16-week point. After that, things ramped up. It seemed that the beings I was carrying were now irretrievably committed. Committed to *me*, committed to this life we were going to enter together. Other mothers have had different experiences. If science ever gives us an answer, I will be highly skeptical of it.

For me: the kids arrived, full force, not gradually. There were hints of a pregnancy, hints of personality, food cravings specific to each child (highly exotic and spicy for Jacob, macaroni and cheese for Julian), dreams in which one was a physicist and the other a musician. There was a line, though, or at least a zone, somewhere along the way from hints at who these children would be to when I knew they were *there*. When the thing that disappears after a death arrives in a life. Perhaps a soul has dibs on a certain mother, a certain fetus. It floats attached by some longer cord, waiting to see if there will be a miscarriage or an abortion. Gauging. And then, wham, the cord reels in. For better or worse that soul is inside a body inside you.

I wonder if the question of a human soul is less pressing on mothers than on men in general. I wonder if the whole idea that souls might *not* exist is something that's been posed by men, and sometimes adopted by women, as many of the questions and beliefs of men have been adopted by women in direct contradiction to their "irrational"—i.e., not perceived by men—personal experiences.

Of course, it's not irrational at all to rely on personal experiences. A combat veteran may have the reflexes necessary to sidestep a mugging well before there is any overt hint that the assailant means him harm. Intuition goes deep into our human and pre-human wiring. It's probably embedded in our rat, lizard, and bird brains, the substrates on which our more modern cerebral cortices rest. While it's a bit simplistic to say that these pre-human parts of our brains are located in one place, such as the limbic center (elements are actually distributed throughout our brains), they do continually supply the more complex, "rational" parts with information. The thing is, our pre-human receptors "think" faster than the supposedly smarter parts of us can. They draw on information not accessible to rational analysis—information we may ignore at our peril. The smell of a predator, a certain sound mixed in with a lot of background noise, a flicker in a shadow. This is what the rat-brain perceives. And it knows comfort when it feels it. A truly rational brain incorporates what its other parts are telling it. It might reject some of this information for good reason. It might say, Look: there are no pterodactyls anymore, so we need not be alarmed, as it turns out some people are, by the shadow of a swooping wind turbine. But in my opinion, the skepticism of those who are closed to their own pre-human cognitions is not in itself good reason for rejecting our intuitions. It's silly to ignore the feeling you're being watched, for instance. There are lions in the woods where I live. There are stalkers in the cities.

Intuition may in some cases be cellularly based. Many of our reactions to various physical stimuli may be embedded in our DNA and expressed through epigenetics. In *Surviving Survival*, Laurence Gonzales discusses many of the implications of the rat-brain's perceptions I've included above. He brings up the particular intimacies a pregnant mother shares with her unborn child, as their cells mix in her bloodstream. Part of her child's body flows with that blood into her own brain, and some of her brain cells mix with the child's. Who knows what the entire brains of these enmeshed individuals may be capable of decoding about each other?

My "intuition" told me my first child was destined for greatness. I'm sorry if that sounds self-serving and even typical. What came through in the dreams, even in the waking moments when I'd hike a trail near our house and let my thoughts wander, was that this child was driven, determined, ready to take on life.

But my intuition had another message for me, one which contradicted the first so profoundly that I felt I had no choice but to ignore it. Gonzales discusses this dismissal of intuition also, calling it "the tyranny of the rational mind." At around five months, when I felt sure of Jacob's soul-presence, I had a disturbing dream. A young, ambitious boy was carrying luggage for his idol, a mentor and a teacher, whom he hoped to emulate and surpass one day. The boy fell into a pond. The luggage dragged him down to its bottom. He fought. He tried to break free and swim to the surface, but it was too late. He drowned.

At the bottom of the pond, he entered a cave. A bearded, white-robed man came in, examined the boy, made a notation on the clipboard. I, who had been an observer up to this point, passionately pled—there was so much the boy wanted to do with his life! But the man with the clipboard laughed in my face. The boy was to die, and nothing could change that.

I recorded the dream in my journal, without connecting it to my pregnancy. In retrospect that seems so hard to believe. The water, the cave: classic symbols of the womb. I'd taken enough religious studies classes in college to know this even then. The ambition I'd felt burning so strongly within the child I carried was there in the dream, too. I woke up grieving, raging.

Then I forgot the whole thing. I was astounded to re-encounter this dream when, shortly after Jake's death, I read back through my journal entries for the months of the pregnancy. The feeling when that man with the clipboard *laughed* in my face…it so exactly prefigured what I felt when fate took my child, who in turn had seemed fated to accomplish so much in this world. Destiny had shifted. A notation on a clipboard, just like the doctor made in real life. Time of death.

A subjective experience. Just a dream. There were other ways to interpret it. Perhaps I tried at the time. It was one of those atmospheric dreams that I always record in my journal, the kind that resound with significance, even if you can't decode it.

I say I don't exhaust myself with building a narrative around experiences and beliefs, but that isn't entirely true. I clung to certain beliefs. I believed my son was healthy and brilliant. He was certainly robust; I could feel that physically. I believed I was destined to be his mother. I knew we were soulmates.

But Jacob *did* drown. His destinies became incompatible with one another. It felt as though God or the universe or fate were laughing in our faces.

After he died, I became friends with Liz Caile, a woman beloved in our community, known for her commitment to nature, for living in a wind-powered cabin you had to hike to. She wrote a column in our town's weekly paper and shopped at the natural food co-op where I volunteered. Liz and I had been hello-saying acquaintances during my first pregnancy, with an occasional confidence passed over the counter as I rang up her beans and organic vegetables.

After a major trauma, the landscape of your relationships changes. Some of your best friends, people you thought would be there through anything, drop out of contact entirely. New friends come out of the woodwork. Liz had been a woodwork dweller. We shared a lot: parenting concerns, though her kids were much older; writing; deep intuitive responses to the natural world; and, it turned out later, a mental illness neither of us recognized as such during her lifetime. She became like a grandmother to my second child.

Then she died, at 54, of a secret cancer. It had, as kidney cancer can, disguised itself for years as something else. In her case it appeared to be rheumatoid arthritis, which ran in her family. Pain built. Even before the pain became crippling, she wrote stories about women creeping into the wilderness to die, climbing into trees, hiding in watersheds, being consumed by lions. Finally, the cancer came out of its woodwork, too late for anything to be done. "I believe," her husband told me, "that some people are so attuned to their bodies they sense something wrong long before it's symptomatic. The doctors couldn't find it, but Liz knew it was there." I think now of the ankle that ached weeks before I broke it, the unexplained hip pain in my teens that reappeared in my forties and forced a serious surgery. A bone hadn't grown in right, though the doctors of my adolescence rolled their eyes and told me it was psychosomatic.

When she was dying, Liz was unable to communicate much to me. "It's hard work, letting go," she said. "All your life you're losing bits of your ego, things not turning out the way you thought. Discovering you're not that special. And now, whatever scraps you've held onto are being wrenched away." Though she'd had some work published in literary magazines, she left behind poems, essays, stories in various states of completion. And she always said her journals were her best work.

Once, when I was sitting beside her with Julian, who was six, she woke violently, sitting up, gasping. "I can't help you," she said after catching her breath, although I hadn't expected any help. We were just sitting, being present. I was hoping to be there for *her*. I suppose she intuited my deep, unexpressed need, though. To know what death, not dying, was like. "This isn't any fun. But I want you to know there's this wonderful baby who keeps appearing." Though she had ended pregnancies amidst considerable emotional pain, she didn't think this child was one of those. She thought he was *my* son. Dead, then, nine years.

Bewildered, but I suppose also hopeful, I wrote down what she said. Liz was dying with enormous potential still unrealized. That was also a large part of my dream about the pond and the guy with the clipboard. The pain the child felt in the dream, the pain I felt watching him, was about what could never come to pass in his life or mine. The relinquishment of his goals and drive. The laughter of the man with the clipboard was the indifference of the universe, the finality of death, the part of his fate that could not be changed. Life tearing away the ego, death devouring the remainder. Perhaps it's how we all die. Perhaps, though, the differential is steeper for some people. What you haven't been able to get done looms over you. Maybe Jake, or some representation of him, *had* come to Liz, to help her with this nasty math problem.

Who knows how time works in the afterhere. Perhaps in some way, Liz was coming for Jake, as well. It seemed he was so alone, not in leaving, but in where he went.

Many babies with Jake's condition quietly fade into death. Their hearts grow weaker, their blood backs up, their arms and legs turn blue and curl in toward their torsos. Perhaps they murmur and squeak the way babies do as they sleep. They might cry a little.

Jacob fought. He *was* a fighter. As his heart was shutting down, which happened in waves separated sometimes by hours of quiescence, he yelled. He threw back his head. He yelled, a deep alarum. Anything alive fights death, but the level of his struggle sunk us, sunk the hospital staff. Again the dream, watching the boy with big goals fight against drowning. The same fight, the same inevitable cessation. There was nothing to be done, except hold him, love him.

Of course, I questioned our decision, now irrevocable. Perhaps he did want to fight, after all. Over time, I came to feel that he fought for the life, the love, we'd given him. Had we given him a different life, he might have slipped off gently into the night. None of this slim consolation was available in the moment, watching him wage a battle that could not be won.

A new dilemma arose. Obviously, Jake was in a lot of pain. The nurse offered morphine. I hadn't slept more than a few hours in three days; the introduction of anything new paralyzed me. "Will it kill him?" I asked. She thought it might. I wanted the moment of his passing to be Jake's own choice. Though I was dim about what an infant could comprehend, I sensed this much—that Spirit should decide the hour. I also knew that morphine would distort his last experience of life on earth. On the other hand, his suffering was awful to behold. I knew that agony, too, could distort the end of his life. I didn't want to deny him the release from pain that we would offer to, say, a dog. In the end there was a suppository. I can't remember if it contained morphine or only Tylenol.

I'd never, then, read any hospice literature. As Jacob lay along my thigh during one of his quiet periods, breathing just lightly, sometimes pausing long moments between breaths, the nurse came into the room. My back was toward the door, my husband was turned toward me. There was a change in the air as the door to our private hospital room opened and she stood quietly inside the room, just watching, respecting the moment we were in. I didn't turn; I was focused on my son's slowing breaths. I assumed she would come forward when we asked her to.

My baby son took his last breath, a small gasp. I waited who knows exactly how long. Time stretched. No breaths followed. In a panic, I turned to the nurse.

There wasn't a nurse. The door was closed. And now my son was vacant too.

That feeling of being watched. It's been essential to our survival as a species. It would be stupid to ignore it.

I always knew I'd meet survivors. Statistically the chances were against it, but I'm an attractor for seemingly significant signs and synchronistic encounters. One morning a stag, a hart, shot through the breast with an arrow, died beneath my bedroom window. On my wall I had Frida Kahlo's The Wounded Deer, a self-portrait in the body of a stag pierced with fletched arrows. What did it all mean? Why, out of all the woods available to die in, had the animal come to me? It had run a mile after it was shot. I'd just finalized my divorce, my eight-year-old son said he wished he could die, his older brother was already dead, and of a heart defect. We were heartshot.

So, if things like that could happen, if, in a six-month period, there had been *two* other families with one-out-of-a-hundred-thousand HLHS deaths in our grief group, why shouldn't I run across rare children with heart transplants, or with hearts that have been replumbed to run on one side only?

When we decided not to replace or "fix" Jacob's heart, we knew that the technology would advance. Maybe even some of the unknown kids from Jacob's cohort would make it. One day we'd run across or hear of HLHS survivors. And when we did, how could we not second-guess?

When these meetings happened, though, I was surprised at the kinds of questions that arose for me.

I was on an annual gourmet picnic hike with my second husband, meeting up with friends. We were late, so we'd brought only dessert, while those ahead of us dined on china, using silver to cut into poached salmon and parmesan risotto cooked on-site. Due to violent Rocky Mountain fall weather, some of the hikers had left early. We found the remainder huddled in the woods. The only people toughing it out were the organizers and a family we hadn't met before. The star of the day was a fiery little girl, eighteen months old. If her face seemed a little rounder than usual, if her chest was distended more than other toddlers', if despite her energy and laughter she was very pale, it didn't strike me as outside the norm.

"She's our miracle baby," one of her uncles said tipsily, proudly. "This baby had a heart transplant when she was six months[3] old."

Julian and I froze. "Why did she need a transplant?" I asked after a few seconds.

The mother said, "She was born with a rare heart defect."

---

[3] It might have been six weeks.

Obviously. "Which one?"

"She had something called hypoplastic left heart," the mother explained reluctantly. "It's where—"

"I know," I said.

When we met this little girl, fifteen years had passed for me. So, we talked a little, though I thought the mother didn't really want to. In fact, I ran into her again, at a party about ten years later, and though her husband said, "Honey, these are the people we met at the picnic, who had—" she said, "I remember that conversation. We're not going there tonight." Which was too bad. I'd have liked to have learned how their daughter was doing. The father made one mention, later in the evening, of the fact that they couldn't travel anywhere. I didn't know, and felt uncomfortable asking, if they couldn't travel because they were waiting for a new heart, or because they needed to be near a hospital at all times. At two, their daughter was on only a single anti-rejection medication. The mother thought eventually she might not need any medications. I wasn't sure she was being realistic, but she said, "They've come such a long way."

Perhaps they had. Years before, an ICU nurse at Children's Hospital in Denver had said to another HLHS couple in our grief group: "that shit they offer you doesn't work." This was a few years after Jake's death, and after Children's Hospital had launched its own transplant center. Nurses, it seemed to us, would know, better than doctors, how things worked out for the kids. One of my big disappointments regarding the book *Walk on Water* was that it included so few nursing perspectives.

On the mountainside, I asked the other mother about the current expectations for the life of a transplanted heart. She said she'd never heard about any of that. Her daughter was healthy, would stay healthy. I wasn't sure what to believe. The family's optimism, or the facts and figures I'd dug up over the years, when I returned periodically to the archives for updates. I went to libraries in universities and hospitals to look up reports in medical journals. Now, it's a quick Google search. Nowadays: It is still not clear how long the organs themselves last, but it does seem to be longer in children. Kids who survive at least 15 years past a transplant surgery: 54.3 percent, according to a study from Loma Linda Hospital in Los Angeles. More than half! At that rate, the study's authors trumpeted, transplants should be vigorously promoted. The study did not much discuss the 45.7 percent of children who did not survive for 15 years. Nor did it explore the quality of the lives of the survivors. How many with strokes or other permanent damage from the surgery? And always that deep silent pool of babies drowned before a heart became available.

One recent article dismissed the weight of the negatives in seeking a transplant because patients in this condition will die otherwise.

In the end, statistics are meaningless. It's just your kid and his or her fate, resilience, who knows what else. Our chances of having a child with HLHS were 1/100,000, but in our case, of course, they turned out to be 100 percent. Jacob's chances of surviving into adulthood—well, even today, no one knows. Jacob personally either had a 100 percent chance of making it, or a zero percent chance. And that's always the bottom line. It either rains today or it doesn't, regardless of whether my phone app says there is a 30 percent chance.

Enter the third consideration. You can actively choose zero. That is, if you're told that zero is an option. We can't know if the surgeries are more successful, now, considering that most parents want their children to outlive them, not just to survive for 15 years. They're more commonly performed, though, and more children get through more of the stages than have in the past. Doctors today can be reluctant to discuss a sure course toward death.

Not long ago, skiing, I met the sister of a friend. Back at my friend's house, I met her son, a boy of about 16 who had been born with one of the other two always-fatal heart defects. He hadn't gone through the first-phase procedure, Norwood, which Jacob might have faced, but he had ended his sequence with what's called the Fontan procedure, as Jacob might have if we'd taken the surgery route. A transplant was next for this boy.

During one of the early phases of his surgical journey, this child had a stroke on the operating table. He could still communicate and walk, with a limp. He was an intelligent, wryly funny teenager who loved to snowboard and play chess. The combination of the stroke damage and the medications, including steroids, made his life difficult to navigate in many ways. Yet, like the little girl at the picnic, he was *there*. He was a personality. He was smart.

The mother said one of the challenges for their family was that she and the father did not agree on whether and when to intervene medically. "We have that discussion again, every time there's a new procedure." She said if one parent felt strongly that they should fight, you had to go with that. Her boy died at 21, of a type of lymphoma, one of the complications that can arise in transplant recipients (others include transplant rejection, heart failure due to accelerated coronary plaque buildup, and kidney failure). By then he'd had years of a relatively good life mixed in with the surgery and illness. "I loved our life, because it was ours," his mother recently emailed me.

Both of these mothers of survivors got to hear their children laugh. What wouldn't I give for that? The echo of Jake's laughter in my ears.

I used to watch other kids the same age as my Jake would be. As my second son began to grow up, I could see how some of my early impressions from the womb found their places in his personality. This gave me confidence regarding my sense of who Jake was. For several years I would project where Jacob too might have been as they played together, 20 months apart in age. With the passage of more time, years, divergences appeared. My second son buried some of what I thought were his key traits, adopted others. He's 30 now, and the infant is not so easy to identify within the man.

Randall Jarrell wrote a strange persona poem embodying a woman who had lost two children, one to death, the other to adulthood. "It is strange/To carry inside you someone else's body;/To know it before it's born;/.../You are the authority upon it." Yet, as the surviving daughter grows, "Little by little the child in her dies." When the mother dreams of the daughters, both alive, playing together, she awakes, delighted. "I've seen them again, and I am comforted/That somewhere, they still are." She says "the fair one..../is lost just as the dark one, who is dead, is lost." But the world where they are both wearing their little coats and matching hats "exists so uncannily." I didn't like this poem when I read it in high school, and I still don't think it's Jarrell's best work. But he nails that sense of disorientation, that mystery in contemplating children who have left you for their own paths.

I thought for sure Jacob would grow into the flattering fate that Emerson said, "seemed to say/This child should ills of ages stay/By Wondrous tongue and guided pen/Bring the flown muses back to men." As I raised my second son among his peers and alongside mine, I came to see that most children do not exactly grow into their parents' dreams for them. I had believed that my second child was sensitive, artistic, musical, resistant to enclosure. Much of this turned out to be true. He played violin—with perfect tone—when he was younger, could pick out tunes by ear on the piano and guitar. He now composes music, though, as it turns out, he's the physics major. He told me I could only hug him till he was ten, and he pushed me away much earlier than that. He ran away briefly when he was fifteen. He loves animals and would flinch visibly when we came upon something destructive to nature—greenbelt being carved into subdivisions, a pile of uranium tailings. During the pregnancy I thought he might be a girl. I wish I was a girl, he said at age seven, uncomfortable with the roughhousing and troublemaking of the boys in his class, with their parroting of their fathers' sports fandom. I think I'm *like* a girl, he said, because I like beauty so much. I mean, I *really* love for things to be beautiful. This soul had its own, separate destiny. That fact seemed clear while I was pregnant with him.

Things changed as he grew, is what I mean to say. The core characteristic of sensitivity and devotion to beauty made him vulnerable to damage following the divorce. Because he couldn't see a life with the violin—and was nearly crippled with performance anxiety—he thrust this instrument, which he loved, away. Not long after Jake died, I dreamt that he was doing bong hits in a carful of teenagers on the dirt road above our house. A destiny I hadn't imagined, though I hadn't exactly been an angel of a teen, myself. Julian similarly took paths I hadn't expected, struggling, despite his gifts, with anxiety and depression.

Raising children for real is humbling, whether they live or die. I only had enough to go on to be able to say for sure that a distinct person appeared inside me one day and was born to the world. Beyond that, I have no idea who he would have become. I no longer have the comfort of imagining him into the future, guessing with any degree of confidence as to who he might be today. That's a grief, too.

And Deep Heart answered, Weepest thou?
    Yes, and still. Days and days per month per season per year.
    How else would you have it? Would you have him live with an-other's heart, or half a heart? Ah, here is a crux in the matter, a curve whose slope is too complicated for any calculus I know of. Had we taken the surgical route—for shorthand, let's just refer to all the sur-gical options as "transplant," since we most likely would have ended up there. Today, as I mentioned, not all small children waiting for a heart get one. Back then, the numbers were unavailable and so, mostly, were the hearts. Plus, I thought there was just something grotesquely mechanical about the whole hack-and-splice mentality toward keep-ing people alive. I'm not an extremist. A neighbor's daughter needed a kidney. Ultimately the mother donated one to her. That girl had suf-fered mightily until the age of five, enduring dialysis treatments from the age of two. Her first transplant had failed. Now she is a vibrant young woman with a career she is passionate about. A miracle? No, but a fine feat.
    I am not talking about a parent donating an organ to a child. When Jake was still on life support, he seemed so pale, so weakened, and frankly so miserable, that no one thought he would live long enough for a dead baby's heart to be found. However, when we removed the tubes and needles, he rallied immediately. We hoped we might have some time with him. Perhaps a chance to take him home. At least to take walks in the park near the hospital, get fresh air on his skin. After a day filled with interaction—delight in his baths, coos and babyfaces, hours of eye contact, he began to falter, curling his arms into his body and weeping in pain.
    As he failed, I felt a horrible wrath, a despair, a keening, bursting from my own chest. Hack and splice, sure. I would have let them cut out my heart if it would have cured my son.
    It would not have.
    A transplant is no cure. As medical ethicist Arthur Caplan put it,

"It's a procedure that basically takes you from an acute illness—one that's going to kill you—and turns you into a chronic illness patient."

For a baby with a transplant, you are talking, as another HLHS parent said, about "a 100 percent unnatural life. From day one."

Who is an infant with a heart transplant? While most of the more dramatic accounts of changed personalities following organ transplants have been debunked, the public has been fascinated by urban legends such as the mild-mannered 70+ person with a teen heart who suddenly wants a Corvette, or the girl in India who received a heart from a child who had been murdered, and who allegedly was able to identify the murderer thereafter. I think this says something about what we intuitively feel about our bodies. The mechanism of cellular memory has recently begun to come to light. It involves gene proteins and—again—epigenetics. Meanwhile, somatic therapists have applied the concept of cellular memory to address trauma for decades. I can tell you: that shit *does* work.

In an adult transplant recipient, there is plenty of existing cell memory, there's a developed personality to make decisions about which new inputs to accept or reject.

For myself, I find the idea of transplanted body parts grotesque. My donor card excludes the major organs. I do not want big pieces of me living on in other peoples' bodies.

I'll never know how much of this squeamishness, perhaps even superstition, affected my decision. In another life, or in another moment of this life, I might have been more open. Body and soul forge personhood together. Change *anything* congenitally, even the shape of a foot, and you have a different person. In a different life trajectory, I might well have opted for adopting a child. At that particular moment, though, I didn't want to raise any other baby. The person I wanted to raise was not some pastiche of re-tied arteries and strangers' organs, but the being I made with my own body.

That being was born unable to live.

Weepest thou? Yes, and still.

There were other left-field discoveries. Between 1990 and 1995, Rick Strassman, a tenured professor at the University of New Mexico, studied the effects of N,N-dimethyltriptophan (DMT), which can trigger near-death experiences, among other things. He gave 400 doses to 60 volunteers. Research support came from diverse sources, including the National Institute of Health and what he calls "flexibility" from the Food and Drug Administration and the Drug Enforcement Agency. What drew him to this study, he says, was the natural availability of DMT in all our bodies. He wondered why we had it. His approach, which was to interweave speculative conclusions with discussion of his own motivations, "will satisfy no one.... There is intense friction between what we know intellectually, or even intuitively, and what we experience with DMT. ...As Dogen, a thirteenth century Japanese Buddhist teacher, said, 'We must always be disturbed by the truth.'"

Disturbed I was.

Strassman's research is the largest body of data regarding impacts and effects of DMT. Some of his stated "speculations" have been challenged, unfairly it seems to me, as being, well, speculative. For example, his thoughts on where DMT originates in the body and whether it, or a combination of endorphins, are responsible for the experiences labeled as near-death experiences. One researcher argues that the levels of DMT injected by Strassman's team were far higher than could be accounted for by the levels naturally occurring in the brain (or body, because it's also present in cerebrospinal fluid, and who knows, maybe the gut, since now it's thought that so much of what goes on in the brain has a link to the intestines).

Strassman's book, *The Spirit Molecule*, affected me deeply when it came out in 2001. Because of what Strassman reported—and *speculated*—I began to be uncomfortable with some of our decisions. Not so much the surgery versus no-surgery choice. Instead, I worried that we hadn't had a funeral or an appropriate wake. Strassman says DMT is present before birth. It remains active in the brain for hours or days after death. He believes a release of DMT from the pineal gland at about 10 weeks marks the entrance of the soul into the fetus.[4]

Recreational users of DMT have reported NDEs, out-of-body experiences, alien abductions (strikingly common with the higher dos-

---

[4]The proposal that DMT is manufactured in the pineal—poetic because of René Descartes's reflection that the pineal must be the seat of the soul—is under debate.

es Strassman administered), and travels to far sides of the universe. Endogenous dumps of this substance could be behind some mystical experiences, and unlike many reductive researchers, Strassman does not say they are therefore not "real." He suggests that in some cases higher levels of DMT may help people access those experiences—and some people, such as shamans and people with schizophrenia, may have higher levels to begin with. Note that DMT is one of the primary psychotropic ingredients in ayahuasca, an Amazonian plant-based psychedelic. Drinking ayahuasca tea is lately a worldwide ceremonial phenomenon. As one participant said, ayahuasca showed her the difference between who she thought she was, and who she really was. Her insights were agonizing, but the pain precipitated for her a long period of growth and change.

So, what is DMT *doing* inside us? Strassman asks. Why do we naturally make it? Perhaps, as some have argued, it makes death and severe trauma easier to manage. If you leave your body during a cardiac arrest, the resulting distanced view may help you survive until your body responds. By you, I don't just mean your physical survival, but the *you* of you, your point of view and consciousness. Strassman suggests—I was going to say argues, but in spite of all his good work, it would be hard to support such an argument, given that many don't even believe in the soul—that DMT is the spirit molecule. He says it's a tool, a means of accessing the spiritual, the mystical, the multi-dimensional, the higher states of meditation, sexual transcendence, and even the demonic.

A tugboat, drawing the soul into the body, then out when death arrives.

Perhaps, as Strassman says, the reason for such rituals as vigils and wakes, the careful preparations for the grave, the emphasis on burials instead of cremation found among some cultures, is to allow DMT to complete its work after "death," so that the soul can leave the body on its own terms rather than on a schedule set by funeral directors. Rituals shaped by intuition, again, and anciently. Even just 75 years ago, American women traditionally bathed, dressed, and laid out a corpse for burial. Friends, neighbors, relatives might drop by to view the body or just to sit with those in mourning. Recently, a mentor of mine described sitting at her mother's deathbed and then keeping vigil beside her beautifully displayed body for a couple of days. By the time it was necessary to bury the body, she said, her mother had gone from peaceful-looking to radiant.

Until more work is done in this area, I have no trouble seeing DMT as Charon's ferry. My fear is that because of our ignorance, Jacob missed his ride.

After Jake died, we left the hospital room, *fled* it. We left the terrible shell of his body. That moment when life—not just the breath or the heartbeat, but the soul—exited. We fled that.

We were just beginning our adult lives. We had no pastor, not even someone to mouth the platitudes. We were too proud for that, anyway, unable to bear the clichés. We took what had meaning—toys sent by well-wishers, clothing that smelled of him, foot and hand prints, a lock of hair. We fled into the strange, muffled world known to bereaved parents, which Aleksandar Hemon has called "The Aquarium," where we were to drown for years yet. The airlock to this place was the drive through Boulder Canyon, 30 miles and 3000 feet of elevation gain, filled with people rock climbing, hiking, and driving their own cars as if it were a normal day.

We had become a statistic. Somewhere in your community there is another one, a baffled, riven family emerging from a hospital, leaving behind the flesh of their child, dead of a rare disease.

The next day, as relatives began to arrive, my son's coldness began to torment me. I'd brought a special outfit to the hospital, something handmade of organic cotton, but I'd left him wrapped in only the thin hospital blanket. I wanted to go back, dress him, tuck him in.

We visited the funeral home. The director was a neighbor and greeted us at the door on a Saturday with a bear hug. I remember that.

They had him in a Styrofoam box. That was a shock. Of course, we hadn't specified otherwise. No one had mentioned picking out a coffin. To be honest, it seemed silly to spend money on a coffin for the oven.

He was more blue from the cyanosis than I had remembered, which made him look as if he *felt* the cold. He was frozen stiff. The simple act of dressing him would have broken his bones. Perhaps that's

47

what undertakers do, if you buy the coffin. Or pay to use the facilities and the generic chaplain for a funeral.

I think perhaps my husband's parents tried to encourage us to go through with the generic funeral. I think we were too tired and too confused to even answer them.

I regret: not having that funeral anyway, no matter how canned, clichéd, and completely alien to our beliefs, or lack of them. I regret not *knowing* that we should. We had taken all this care that Jacob have a gentle death. We had enough intuition to get that far. But when it came to supporting his soul in its exit, we had fled.

Because we didn't want any distractions during Jacob's life and death, we had refused most requests from friends and neighbors to visit us in the hospital. We asked family not to come. They would not have arrived in time, we thought. And they were a very needy tribe, always struggling with migraines, sinuses, sleep, directions. Usually quite vocal about the discomforts of travel and being away from home. We felt they would require more attention than we could give them.

Maybe not. Maybe we should have given them a chance to shine for us. Maybe it would have enriched Jacob's short life, all our lives, had we been more open. Maybe someone would have had some ideas to help us.

Meanwhile, Jake went to the flames perhaps before he was fully dead. I don't mean that he suffered more in any earthly way, just that perhaps he hadn't died to his life on earth. Perhaps he'd had his body and its residue of DMT destroyed before the spirit molecule had done its work. I mean that some of these rituals—bedside vigils, ceremonies quoting the same old Psalm, keening—are not just for the living but also for the dead. I mean that, as Waldorf education founder Rudolf Steiner thought, some of the particular agony of a child's death may stem from the grief of the child. His sense of loss and rage at leaving us, leaving life on earth.

We left him in the hospital, left him in the morgue, left him in the fire.

In English it's not possible to make a statement containing a double negative. It seems to be an algebra problem. He who ain't got no heart technically has one. Russian, which I studied for seven years, negates everything. *Nikovo nikogda nigde nichevo ne bylo.* In English: No one was ever there. But more literally: *No one was nothing, not ever, not anyplace.* English worries about the math. Russian is concerned with *nyet*.

Nyet, said the doctor-god of my nightmare, making his notations. *Cyn ne yest. Ne byl, ne budyet.* Your son is not. He wasn't, he won't be.

Take the right side of the heart, replumb it, reshape it, leaving half a heart. Two working chambers, no matter how tricked out, are fewer than four. Or take the whole heart, replace it with one belonging to another, belonging to another mother's heart, made by her blood, her womb, her placenta. One heart where there should be two. New hearts gobbled up down the road, if there is a road. Or provide comfort care: love your baby to death, which like any heart failure, will be crushingly painful.

Never take him home. Never hear him laugh.

An awful choice between a worst thing and another worst thing.

If two negatives don't produce a positive, then we're in some undiscovered part of the graph. This is the kind of thing where people say, "no words." Perhaps what they mean is no grammar. Or just not the right language in which to speak the words. He ain't got no heart. His heart is hidden, unknown. Jacob isn't anyplace, and never was not.

ACKNOWLEDGMENTS

Thank you to Jacob, for being in my life. Thank you to Julian for staying in my life. Thanks to their father, John Putnam, for them. Thanks, as always, to Tony Passariello. Thanks to Phillips Exeter Academy; I began some sections of this project during a residency there. Thank you, Margo Steeves and Kathleen Hurley.

Huge thanks to Lauren Westerfield, David Wojciechowski, Kristine Langley Mahler, Caleb Tankersly, Allison Renner, Emmy Newman, and the rest of the extremely organized, passionate, and diligent team at Split/Lip Press, and to Jenny Boully for selecting *Double Negative* as the chapbook winner for 2021.

Readers: Special thanks to Kristin Carlson, Marko Fong, and David Weber. James Marcus and Mairead Small Staid. And to the Glenwood Springs Writers' Group—we were just digging into the opening sections when Covid hit, but you helped.

Thanks to Juliet Wittman, who published my first attempt to be articulate about this experience in Boulder's *Sunday Camera Magazine* all those decades ago.

Thanks to the communities of Eldora and Nederland, CO, which held us so tightly during the loss described in this book, and then embraced and celebrated Julian.

To Albert Mehl, M.D., James Loehr, M.D., and Karen Ferguson, M.D. To the NICU nurses at Boulder Community Hospital and what was then known as University Hospital in Denver (I kept a list of your names for years, but it has not survived the more recent moves and upheavals in my life—I apologize for this, because you were the best).

To the late Liz Caile, to Jean Kindig, and to Jane Wodening for being my muses while I lived in Eldora, whether they knew it or not.

It seems I must thank Ralph Waldo Emerson for the work that has been such a lodestar for me.

To the dogs and cats who have seen me through everything.

And to everyone else who has ever offered a shoulder to cry on, a listening ear, and/or a few cheers. Thanks for your love.

ABOUT THE AUTHOR

CLAUDIA PUTNAM lives in Western Colorado, where she works part-time as a craniosacral therapist. Her prose can be found in *Confrontation*, *phoebe*, *Sunspot Lit*, *bosque magazine*, *Cimarron Review*, and elsewhere. Her debut poetry collection, *The Land of Stone and River*, recently appeared from Moon City Press. She has received several residency awards, including the year-long Bennett Fellowship from Phillips Exeter Academy. She is the mother of two children. Her surviving son, Julian, is a chef in Seattle.

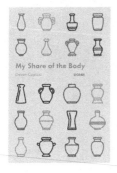

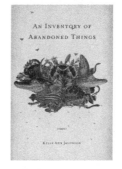

Made in the USA
Monee, IL
10 October 2024

67253348R00036